Jellyfish Shoes

SUSAN GATES

Illustrated by John Prater

OXFORD
UNIVERSITY PRESS

OXFORD
UNIVERSITY PRESS

Great Clarendon Street, Oxford OX2 6DP

Oxford University Press is a department of the University of Oxford.
It furthers the University's objective of excellence in research, scholarship,
and education by publishing worldwide in

Oxford   New York

Auckland   Cape Town   Dar es Salaam   Hong Kong   Karachi
Kuala Lumpur   Madrid   Melbourne   Mexico City   Nairobi
New Delhi   Shanghai   Taipei   Toronto

With offices in

Argentina   Austria   Brazil   Chile   Czech Republic   France   Greece
Guatemala   Hungary   Italy   Japan   Poland   Portugal   Singapore
South Korea   Switzerland   Thailand   Turkey   Ukraine   Vietnam

Oxford is a registered trade mark of Oxford University Press
in the UK and in certain other countries

First published 1998
This edition 2005

British Library Cataloguing in Publication Data
Data available

ISBN-13: 978-0-19-917969-5
ISBN-10: 0-19-917969-7

1 3 5 7 9 10 8 6 4 2

Available in packs
Stage 10 More Stories A Pack of 6:
ISBN-13: 978-0-19-917963-3; ISBN-10: 0-19-917963-8
Stage 10 More Stories A Class Pack:
ISBN-13: 978-0-19-917970-1; ISBN-10: 0-19-917970-0
Guided Reading Cards also available:
ISBN-13: 978-0-19-917972-5; ISBN-10: 0-19-917972-7

Cover artwork by John Prater
Photograph of Susan Gates © Pauline Holbrook

Printed in China by Imago

Laura had some new jelly shoes.

She was really proud of them.
They were pink and see-through like
raspberry jelly.

She ran down to the beach in them.
Wherever she walked, they left little
tracks in the sand.

Like this:

'Look, Scott,' Laura called to her brother. 'My new jelly shoes are leaving stars in the sand.'

Squidge. Laura trod in something slippery. She lifted up her shoe.

'*Ughhh!*' she said. 'What's that mess?'

'It's only a jellyfish,' said Scott. 'The sea washes them up on the beach.'

'Well, I don't like it,' said Laura. 'It looks like a jelly cow-pat.'

Slosh. The sea washed up some more jellyfish. Pink ones this time. They spread out in pink puddles on the sand.

'Watch out,' said Scott. 'Jellyfish can give you a nasty sting.'

'*Yuk!*' cried Laura. 'There are loads of them! And, phew, what a pong! I hate them. They'll spoil my new jelly shoes!'

Scott looked at the jellyfish on the sand. He looked at Laura's new shoes. An idea popped into his head.

'I don't know why you hate jellyfish,'
said Scott. 'What do you think your new
shoes are made of?'

Laura looked down at her shoes. They
were see-through and pink. The jellyfish on
the beach were see-through and pink too.

'Don't be silly,' she told Scott. But her
voice was shaky.

'I thought you knew,' said Scott. 'Don't you know what happens to all these washed-up jellyfish?'

Laura shook her head.

'I'll tell you what happens,' said Scott, who was good at stories. 'The jelly workers come round. They come round at night with bin bags. And they shovel all the jellyfish into the bags. And they take them away to the Jelly Shoe Factory.'

He went on, 'And they make them
into shoes. Just like the ones you've
got on. I thought everyone knew that!'

Laura looked down at her new
shoes.

'I don't think I like my new shoes
any more,' she said.

Then she tore them off.

'*Yuk!*' she said. 'I don't want pongy
jellyfish shoes that sting me!'

She threw them into the sea.

They didn't sink. Jellyfish shoes don't sink. They just bobbed about on the waves. And washed further and further away from the shore.

'Good riddance!' shouted Laura, waving them goodbye.

Then she tiptoed back to the house in her bare feet.

3

That night Laura dreamed about the jellyfish workers. She dreamed they crept along the beach with bin bags in their hands. They bent down and shovelled up jellyfish. Soon they had whole shivering sackfuls of them. Flies were buzzing all around them.

'Oh no!' cried Laura, waking up. 'The jelly workers are coming!'

But it was all right. She was safe in her own bed. 'It was just a bad dream,' she told herself.

Yet down on the dark beach, something was moving. Something was bobbing about on the waves.

It was Laura's jellyfish shoes. They were coming back home.

Gently, they washed in on the wave tops until at last a big wave washed them up on the sand. Neatly side by side.

'What a bit of good luck!' said Mum the next morning. 'Guess what I just found on the beach?'

'Don't know,' said Laura.

Mum held up the jellyfish shoes.
'These! I bet you didn't even know
you'd lost them.'

Mum tipped up one of the shoes.
A winkle fell out of the toe.

'Here you are,' she said, handing the
shoes to Laura. 'You can put them back
on now.'

Laura pushed the shoes away:
'I won't put them back on!' she shouted.
'You can't make me!'

Mum stared at her. 'What on earth is
the matter? I thought you'd be pleased
to get them back.'

'I don't want them. I don't want
smelly shoes that make flies buzz all
around me! Why did you do it, Mum?
Why did you buy me shoes made of
jellyfish?'

And Laura rushed out of the door.

Mum shook her head, puzzled. 'Shoes
made of jellyfish?' she said. 'What's she
talking about? Do you know, Scott?'

'Don't ask me,' said Scott. But he
looked a bit guilty.

Laura rushed down to the beach
without her jellyfish shoes. Scott came
running after her. He had the shoes in
his hand.

'Mum says you've got to put them on.'

'No! I'm never wearing those horrible
shoes again! Not ever!'

'Look,' began Scott. 'There's
something I've got to tell you. What I
said yesterday, about the Jelly Shoe
Factory –'

But he didn't get time to finish.

'What's that?' said Laura. 'What's that in the sea?'

The sea was full of tiny, frilly parachutes. They were pink and brown and purple.

'They're beautiful!' cried Laura. 'What are they?'

'They're baby jellyfish,' said Scott. 'Hundreds of them.'

'Jellyfish!' Laura jumped back.

'And if we don't save them,' said Scott, 'the sea will wash them up. They'll get splatted on the sand. They'll all die.'

'I hate jellyfish!' said Laura. 'They pong. They sting you. They get made into jellyfish shoes.'

'Well, I'm going to save them,' said
Scott. And he raced back to the house.

Laura couldn't help watching the
jellyfish. They sparkled like jewels.
But they were getting closer and closer
to the beach. Soon they would be
dried-up puddles on the sand.

And she couldn't help thinking,
'Poor babies.'

Just then, Scott came racing back
with two buckets. And suddenly Laura
changed her mind.

'I'll help you to save them,' said
Laura. She grabbed a bucket.

'We'll tip them into that rock pool,' said Scott. 'But we've got to hurry!'

'Don't touch them,' he warned. 'Even the babies sting.'

They scooped up the babies in buckets. Then they ran to the rock pool and tipped them in.

'Hurry!' cried Scott. 'The sea's going out!'

Laura dashed to the rock pool. Slosh!
The babies poured out like rainbows.

She ran back again and again. Until
her legs wouldn't work any more.

'I – can't – run – another – step!' she
gasped, sitting down on the sand.

'It's all right,' said Scott. 'Look! The tide's coming in!'

Laura lifted her head. It was true!

'Hurray!' she yelled. 'We've saved them. We saved the jellyfish babies!'

Scott and Laura went to look in the
rock pool.

'It's like jellyfish soup in there!' said
Laura.

'But they're safe,' said Scott. 'And
when the tide comes in, it'll take them
out to the deep, deep sea – where they
belong.'

'I like jellyfish now,' said Laura.
'They're beautiful, aren't they? I'm really
glad we saved them. And now the jelly
workers won't get them. They won't be
taken to the Jelly Shoe Factory and
made into jellyfish shoes.'

Scott looked very guilty.

'I was going to tell you about that,'
he said. 'There isn't any Jelly Shoe
Factory. There aren't any jelly workers.
They don't make jelly shoes out of
washed-up jellyfish.'

'How do you know?' said Laura.

'Because it's just a story. I made it all up!'

'No you didn't!' said Laura.

'I did, I did, honest!' said Scott.

But Laura didn't believe him.

'Where are my jellyfish shoes anyway?' she asked Scott.

Scott looked around. 'I don't know.
I put them down when I went to get the
buckets. They can't have walked off by
themselves...'

Laura looked around too. The beach
was empty. Then she saw a line of
stars, in the sand. They led right down
to the sea.

'There they are!' Scott pointed.

Laura saw her jellyfish shoes. They were bobbing about on the waves. They were heading out to sea.

Scott waded into the water. 'I'm going to get them back!' he said.

29

Laura thought for a minute. Then she said, 'No. Let them go.'

She waved at them. 'Bye bye, jellyfish shoes,' she said, a little sadly.

'What are you going to tell Mum?' asked Scott. 'She'll be very angry!'

But Laura wasn't listening. She was smiling a secret smile. She was thinking about her jellyfish shoes having a lovely time... swimming with whales and dolphins and octopuses... back in the deep, deep sea where they belonged.

About the author

My children gave me the idea for this story. One summer we were on holiday. We were walking along a beach. My daughter, Laura, was wearing a new pair of 'jelly shoes' to paddle in. There had been a big storm the night before and lots of jellyfish were washed up on the beach. My son said, 'Look there's a pink one! It looks like Laura's jelly shoes!' Laura said, 'That's horrible! My shoes aren't made out of jellyfish.' And hey, presto, the idea for *Jellyfish Shoes* was born!